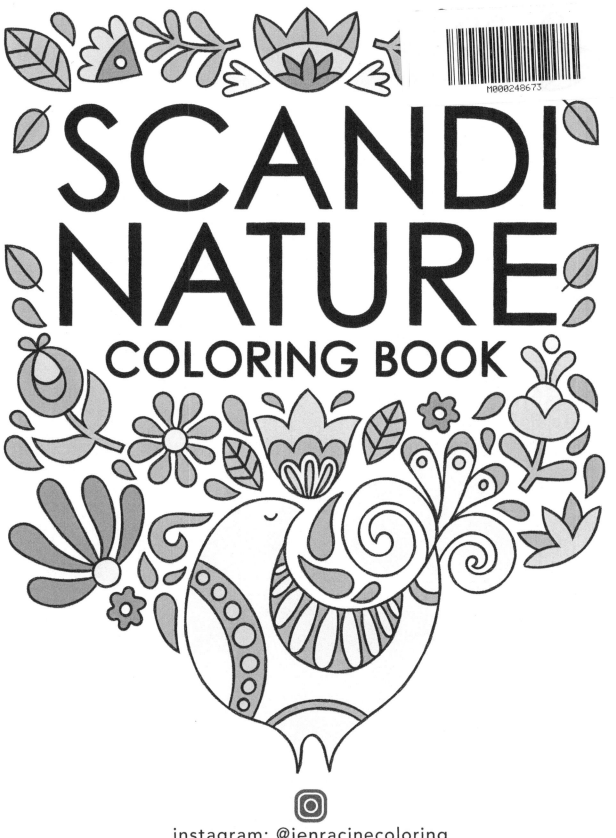

SCANDI NATURE
COLORING BOOK

instagram: @jenracinecoloring

facebook.com/jenracinecoloring

www.jenracine.com

If you like SCANDI NATURE COLORING BOOK, you may like these books by JEN RACINE

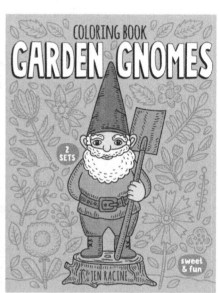

Find coloring pages on Etsy: JenRacineColoring

Copyright © 2020 by Eclectic Esquire Media LLC

ISBN: 978-1-951728-46-5

Made in the USA
Las Vegas, NV
08 June 2023

73126987R00044